Workbook Six
Of the Business Essentials
Series

MEET AND EXCEED

YOUR CLIENTS

EXPECTATIONS

John Millar

ISBN:1536843490
ISBN-13:9781536843491

DEDICATION

I dedicate this book to my mother and father, who raised me while self-employed. They taught me to work hard and listen to everyone but to make my own choices as to what is right and what is wrong.. and oh, did I mention work hard?

Anyone who tells you to work smart not hard hasn't ever done it tough and realized that if you work smart AND hard you will achieve more than you can possibly dream.

CONTENTS

PRODUCT DESCRIPTION

The great belief in the 'loyal customer' who will stay with you for years and refer you to others and help out when times get tough and stand by you through thick and thin – IS A MYTH!

No client can afford to be so doggedly faithful. They have their costs and issues too. These days it's all about how you can be loyal to them! Once you realize that and stop blaming your customers for your own ups and downs, you'll go a long way towards accessing the right thought patterns that will see you through – in all economic climes.

Communicating with them, interacting with their problems, notifying them of changes and events in your business, recognizing their own events, letting them know you're thinking of them – are all significant and important ways in which you instill their regard for you and make them think more than twice before they do business with a competitor.

Your insistence on excellence and consistency will reap its own rewards.

In this DVD we examine and evaluate the factors that contribute to the creation of binding customer relations. We look at several ways in which to KEEP the customers you have whilst attracting new ones to the fold. Some of these ways are obvious and some are hardly ever used – that's why they give you the edge.

Care for your customers. Look after them. Bring them into the family – and they will feel the commitment you have to them. Let's face it – their lives are bombarded daily with thousands of ads, commercials, marketers and calls to action. Yours must be the one they look for – or else.

Regards,

John Millar

How can we get our customers coming back again and again and again and telling everybody to come and see us.

If you never lost a customer, would you ever need a new one?

....

....

....

....

What's customer service?

It's the art of creating raving fans.
here are four different levels of customers within any company.

....

....

....

....

The first customer is the owner

You deserve to get, as a level of customer service, a business that provides you with a fair and equitable level of profit.

....

....

....

....

The second one is the team.

The business has got to serve them by providing them with recognition, rewards, their paycheck, training, development. There are things that you can do to provide great customer service to your team.
Your team are also customers of each other. they're relying on each other to provide a good service to each other both internally and externally.

....

....

The third is our suppliers.

We have to serve them by paying the bills in full and on time. We have to serve them by being able to given them real information and feedback to help them improve their service to us and therefore allowing us to better service our clients.

If we give great customer service to your suppliers you will find that when you ask them for extended trading terms, credit payment details etcetera, they'll be more obliging to look after you because you looked after them.

You've earned the right to ask for that through great customer service.

The fourth is our paying customers.

The business has got to serve them by filling their needs and wants PROFITABLY.

So what is a customer? A customer is someone that I believe buys from you two, three, four, five, or more times.

The business has got to s Remember, we need to grade our customers A, B, C, and D. What are the top 5 characteristics of an A grade client?

1.
2.
3.
4.
5

What are the top 5 characteristics of a B grade client?

1. ....
2. ....
3. ....
4. ....
5 ....

What are the top 5 characteristics of a C grade client?

1. ....
2. ....
3. ....
4. ....
5 ....

What are the top 5 characteristics of a D grade client?

1. ....
2. ....
3. ....
4. ....
5 ....

> Like most businesses you're probably getting 80 percent of your profit from 20 percent of your customers.

Why wouldn't we want to attract more customers who are attracting in the most profit inside your business?

1. ....
2. ....
3. ....
4. ....
5. ....

6. ....

7. ....

8. ....

9. ....

10. ....

> Likewise the ones who were causing 80 percent of the problems and creating 20 percent of your profit should be identified so you can do yourself and do them the favor of introducing them to your competitor.

This way our competitors can enjoy the value and benefit of dealing with those rude clients who are the biggest pains, the worst buyers and those who usually cost you more to do business with than if you removed them from your business.

What are the top 10 characteristics of your least enjoyable and least profitable clients?

1. ....

2. ....

3. ....

4. ....

5. ....

6. ....

7. ....

8. ....

9. ....

10. ....

> How do we take our customers to become a valued member of our business and what does a member really look like?

A member is somebody, is when they've got something that resembles a member's kit and are made clearly able to feel like they belong.

....

....

....

....

Again, if you never lost a customer, would you ever need a new one?

The big problem is a lot of business stop at member or once they become a member stop showing they care.

And like it or not many gyms are a classic example of this failure in their business and set up a rotating door.

They work so hard to get you through the door, selling you up in a membership.
But when you don't use it and you don't renew, then, they don't really care because they're feeling fine at the other end because they often bank on paying members NOT showing up to use their facilities.

Good quality gyms that I've worked with and good quality gyms that I have observed work hard out once they got their members to make sure they stay engaged, that they remain regular, that if they don't come, they get a phone call saying, 'Sally, we missed you. It's been two weeks since you've been to the gym. Is everything okay?

....
....
....
....
....
....

How can you apply this generalized principle specifically within your business?

1. ....
2. ....
3. ....
4. ....
5. ....
6. ....
7. ....
8. ....
9. ....
10. ....

Ultimately, what you're looking to do is to build a long-term relationship with every prospect and client and you can only do that with quality communication.

How often do you keep in contact with your clients beyond an invoice or a blatant attempt to sell them something?

What are the top 10 things that you do to retain and build your relationship with your clients by offering them real value and meaningful contact?

1. ....
2. ....
3. ....
4. ....
5. ....
6. ....
7. ....
8. ....
9. ....
10. ....

> I suggest that you must be in contact with your clients at least every 90 days in a meaningful way.

Make sure that you communicate well as you will then build an emotional bank account with them and they will be more forgiving when you do make a mistake and be more grateful when you do things well.

....

....

....

....

> Remember: All things being equal people would prefer to do business with someone they know, like and trust. All things NOT being equal people will STILL prefer to do business with someone that they know, like and trust!

The more you give, the more you'll get in return.

The reality is deposit often, help often, offer value at all times not just when they're looking to purchase something.

The next stage is we need to move our customers to is an advocate.

....

....

....

....

An advocate is somebody that when asked for a suggestion, will tell somebody about you.

That means that if I'm looking to go to dinner and take my wife and children to dinner in a particular area with a particular cuisine, but if I said to a bunch of people, 'Hi. Look, I'm looking to go to dinner and have a beautiful Indian meal in this particular area; does anybody know the right restaurant?' Then, if other people stick up their hands, 'Look, we all went there. And this particular place was fantastic.' They now become an advocate in your business. That's a really wonderful thing. But unfortunately, they only responded when asked.

Who are your top 10 advocates and what leads you to believe they are strong advocates for you?

1. ....
2. ....
3. ....
4. ....
5. ....
6. ....
7. ....
8. ....
9. ....
10. ....

It's no good to be just good. You need to be truly great. You need to stand out amongst the .

Our goal is to make every client a raving fan. So what's a raving fan?

....

....

....

> A raving fan is somebody who without asking tells everybody about everything that you do. They do your selling for you.

They become your own unpaid sales people.
Can you imagine walking into a barbecue with a bunch of friends and a person walks up
To say this, 'Mike, I'll tell you. Last night, my family and I went into this Italian Bistro. And it was fantastic. You've got to go there. You've got to take the kids. The playground was brilliant. The food was wonderful.'

> Now, that's a raving fan.

Who are your top 10 raving fans and what makes them raving fans?

1.
2.
3.
4.
5.
6.
7.
8.
9.
10.

Take the time to think about what 10 things you can do to change your shoppers to customers and then customers to members?

1.
2.
3.
4.

5. ....

6. ....

7. ....

8. ....

9. ....

10. ....

What can you do to build one step at a time up to a raving fan, your Bs and your As in particular because they are the ones that are going to attract other A & B great clients?

What makes up a raving fan?

Why they got that way?

Why is somebody an advocate and how they got to that level?

What you're going to do to consolidate that membership?

What are the 10 things you need to implement in your business to make these things happen over the next 90 days?

1. ....

2. ....

3. ....

4. ....

5. ....

6. ....

7. ....

8. ....

9. ....

10. ....

An important part of customer service is being proactive and not just reactive.

We got to make sure that we continue to get better and we innovate.

You've heard the term, let's think outside the square? Try these exercises.
Can you connect these 9 dots with 4 straight lines without picking up your pen?

4 Straight lines without picking up your pen

Can you connect these 10 dots with 5 straight lines without picking up your pen?

5 Straight lines without picking up your pen

Can you connect these 10 dots with 5 straight lines without picking up your pen?

5 Straight lines without picking up your pen

Customers will always expect you to get better, to innovate and do something different and that's what those exercises are all about.

> If you don't, it's just the same old, same old.
>
> It's the things that you do beyond a client's expectations that which will set you apart and keep your clients longer, closer and spending more often with you.

1. ....
2. ....
3. ....
4. ....
5. ....
6. ....
7. ....
8. ....
9. ....
10. ....

> So how can you give them more than they can actually expect?

1. ....
2. ....
3. ....
4. ....
5. ....
6. ....
7. ....
8. ....
9. ....
10. ....

What can you do to make it easy for people to buy and do business with you.

1. _____
2. _____
3. _____
4. _____
5. _____
6. _____
7. _____
8. _____
9. _____
10. _____

What can you do to give your clients the wow factor?

1. _____
2. _____
3. _____
4. _____
5. _____
6. _____
7. _____
8. _____
9. _____
10. _____

What gives your clients a feeling of consistency and comfort when they deal with you?

1. ....
2. ....
3. ....
4. ....
5. ....
6. ....
7. ....
8. ....
9. ....
10. ....

What are the things that you can't do consistently that you would like to do consistently.

1. ....
2. ....
3. ....
4. ....
5. ....
6. ....
7. ....
8. ....
9. ....
10. ....

What is it that's really going to make every customer want to be an A-grade customer?

1. ....
2. ....
3. ....
4. ....
5. ....
6. ....
7. ....
8. ....
9. ....
10. ....

What are the things you can do that you need to turn into opportunities to impress?

1. ....
2. ....
3. ....
4. ....
5. ....
6. ....
7. ....
8. ....
9. ....
10. ....

What have you done to be able to improve your customer direction?

1. ....
2. ....
3. ....
4. ....
5. ....
6. ....
7. ....
8. ....
9. ....
10. ....

List as many possible things that you can to improve your moments of truth in the services you do or don't provide.

1. ....
2. ....
3. ....
4. ....
5. ....
6. ....
7. ....
8. ....
9. ....
10. ....

> Think about a short plan on what you're going to do to implement your ideas, who will be doing it, what training or resources they will need and most importantly and by when!

There was a study done in recent years which actually showed why most people actually leave a business and don't return.

People leave because ...

- 1% - Death
- 3% - Move House
- 5% - Buy from a Friend
- 9% - Sold to by a Competitor
- 14% - Product/Price
- 68% - Perceived Apathy

....

....

....

....

....

....

> That the fact remains that you can't be all things to all people all the time but you can help them understand that you care about them and their business.

What do you need to do to make sure you remain engaged with your customers (and team) at all times.

1. ....
2. ....
3. ....
4. ....
5. ....
6. ....
7. ....
8. ....
9. ....
10. ....

How can you apply these principles to you and your business?

1. ....
2. ....
3. ....
4. ....
5. ....
6. ....
7. ....
8. ....
9. ....
10. ....

How can you apply these principles to you and your business?

1. ....
2. ....
3. ....
4. ....
5. ....
6. ....
7. ....
8. ....
9. ....
10. ....

What are you really doing that you need to improve to impress your customers?

1. ....
2. ....
3. ....
4. ....
5. ....
6. ....
7. ....
8. ....
9. ....
10. ....

I promise you, you will achieve the results that you deserve based on what you do or don't do with this information.

John Millar

Answers to the 9 and 10 dot questions that are illustrated above

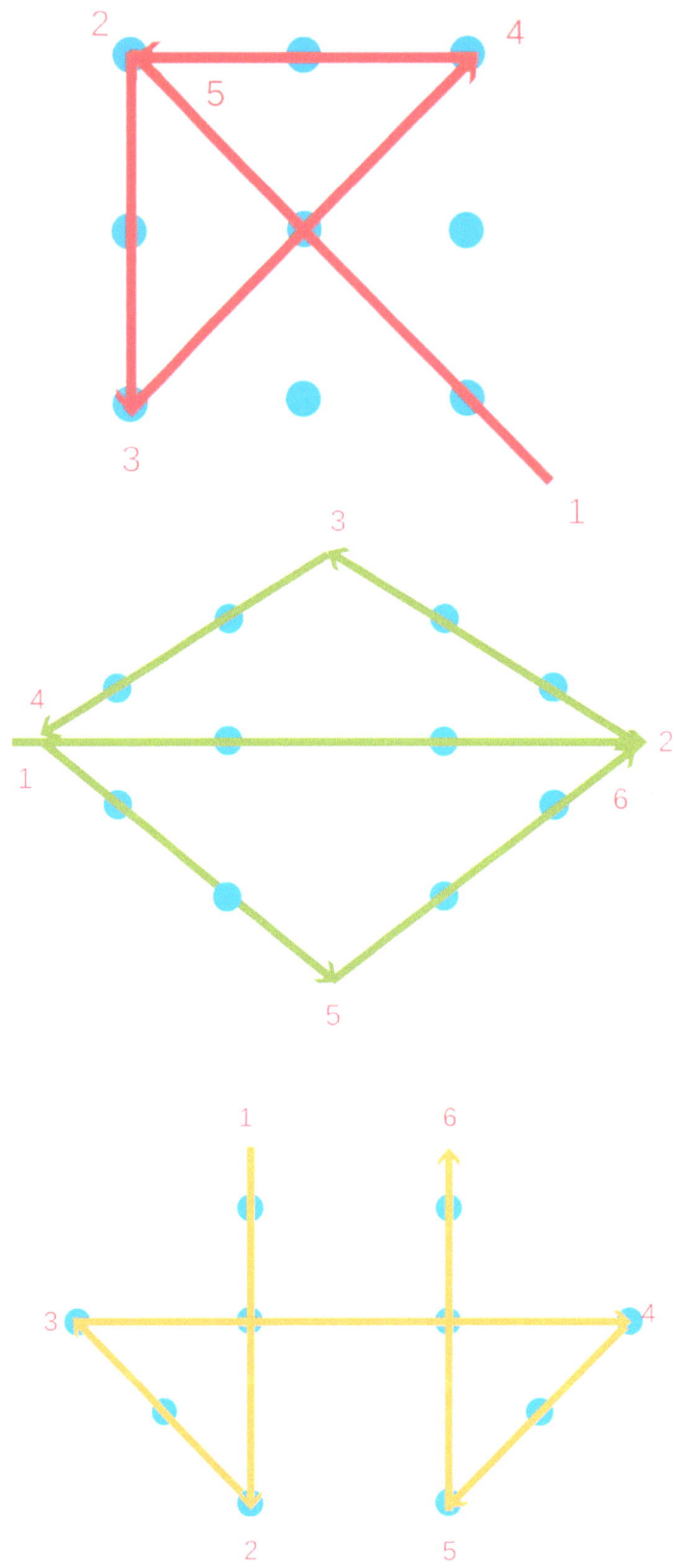

Additional Information to read and consider

Top 10 Ways to Keep Your Customers Happy

The old adage, "it costs five times more to attract a new customer as it does keeping an old one," still holds true today. This simple economics lesson should encourage you to do what you can to keep your customers happy and coming back for return business.

But how can you improve customer satisfaction and retain customers? Here are 10 easy tips you can implement to keeping your customers happy and loyal.

1. Acknowledge customers

Whether by answering a phone call right away, or with eye contact and a simple "I'll be right with you," acknowledging your customers immediately will go a long way in improving customer satisfaction.

2. Know your customers

Literally. Find out their names and greet them by name whenever possible. Get birthday information and send them a special offer or treat on their birthday. This can help improve customer satisfaction by knowing you care about them as individuals.

3. Reward customer loyalty

One strategy to keeping customers happy is to reward them for loyalty. Many businesses have a "buy 5 – get 1 free" card or something similar. Though this is good, you can also reward customers unexpectedly. After a few visits with a return customer, give them a complimentary drink, an added service, or even a gift card.

4. Go the extra mile

Loyal customers like to know you will go the extra mile. If there is a problem, solve the problem and give the customer something extra to let them know they are important to you.

5. Follow up

Customers do not like to follow up for updated information. If you tell a customer you are looking into an issue, be sure to follow up on a regular basis with the status. A phone call or email can make the difference in a happy customer and a disgruntled one.

6. Give special offers to current customers

Use your customer contacts to offer a "members only" type of promotion to current customers. This improves customer satisfaction by making them feel valued and part of an "inside" group.

7. Keep in touch

Try to acquire customer contact information. Then send regular updates via mail or email. A quarterly newsletter is a good way of keeping customers informed of news and simply reminding them of your business name.

8. Differentiate from the competition

Whether you design a creative interior to your retail store or simply provide more value through exceptional customer service, you must keep customers happy by setting yourself apart from your competition.

9. Ask customers for their opinions

What do your customers want? It never hurts to ask customers about their experience and what improvements they would like. This can provide valuable information on how you can improve products and your service delivery.

10. Give samples

Do you have a new product? Current customers can be a good source of market research. Give free samples to existing customers and ask their valued opinion.

Keeping your existing customers happy and loyal is the best way to maintain your company's revenues. In addition, your happy customers will naturally spread the word about your business, which kills two birds with one stone for your long-term growth.

Customer Service PHONE Performance Standards

How poorly do all of our mobile phone message banks and answering skills stack up?

Performance Standard #1
SMILE....until you feel it, BEFORE you pick up the phone

Performance Standard #2
Answer every call AFTER the 2nd ring but BEFORE the third ring

Performance Standard #3
Greet people by saying....
"Good morning/afternoon, thanks for calling <Buz. Name>. This is...<your name>".

Performance Standard #4
Don't screen and always ask permission to put on someone on hold.
Never say a person is 'in a meeting', they are always 'with someone'

Performance Standard #5
Listen attentively and give out positive strokes ("Yes", "I see", "I understand" etc)

Performance Standard #6
Ask Questions irrespective....
• The Magic Question is; "Thanks for your call, just so that I can help you best, would it be OK if I asked you a couple of questions"

Performance Standard #7
Give out little pieces of information and talk in the caller's language

Performance Standard #8
Check the caller's Temperature and ask a detail question
• Temperature: "How does that fit with what you had in mind...?"
• Detail question: "How would you like to pay for that", "When would you like that delivered" etc.

Performance Standard #9
Confirm the order and confirm their Phone Number
• ☺Getting Information: "It's....." (and stay silent!)

Performance Standard #10
Thank your caller

Performance Standard #11
Make sure you hang up LAST, and leave your caller on a HIGH.

What image are you portraying to everyone that does business with you???

How to Use your database. This is YOUR businesses hidden gold mine?

Here's what you can do...

- Send out thank you notes
- Have a closed door or closed fax sale
- Put together a newsletter with special offers in it
- Put together a VIP club or frequent buyers program
- Track your customers buying habits and patterns
- Segment your database into A, B, C and D class clients based on sales volume
- Offer preference packages for past customers to take advantage of
- Offer your top customers a limited number of products first
- Ask your customers to give you referrals
- Notify your customers of sales or specials ahead of the general public
- Send out birthday cards
- Send out Christmas cards and other special occasion cards
- Educate your customers on how you are different so they can understand and appreciate your value
- Run competitions so your customers are continually involved with you and your business
- Direct mail your database with new offers, new products and news in general
- Use your database to test out new offers, new products etc
- Use your database as a source of business for any new business venture you start
- Put on information nights/seminars for past customers
- Sell other people's products and services through your database

To fully utilise your database, simply go through the list above and put together a system for each of the ideas mentioned. You could easily come up with 3 to 4 different variations on each idea. Then take action on each of your ideas.

Remember, test and measure your idea on a small scale first.

Then if it's successful roll it out on a larger scale....

Business Essentials Series...

Disc 1 in the Business Essentials Series
Gaining Focus in Your Business

This is about your fundamental learning skills and what you will need to do to change them to vastly improve the way you look
at your development to become a truly effective business owner not just simply remain self-employed.

You will also give you some excellent tools to set goals, work on your plans and create a diary that will allow you to steal your time back to begin moving your business from chaos to control.

Disc 2 in the Business Essentials Series
Getting Your Financials Right

You will learn the importance of understanding your financials.

After all being in business is about making profit and having cash flow work for YOU since you are responsible for your profits.
Become your accountant and book keepers best friend by understanding more about how the financials in your business works so you can ask them better questions to maximise your profits not simply ensure tax compliance.

Disc 3 in the Business Essentials Series
Leveraging Your Business Harder

You will learn the principles of what and how to leverage far more in your business to get more from less and to work far smarter and not just harder.

Here is where you will receive some of the tools you will need to better understand how to get your business flying, what it is you need to test and measure, how to do it and WHY it's so important.

Disc 4 in the Business Essentials Series
How to Generate More Clients Profitably

This is where you will determine your uniqueness, develop a meaningful guarantee and learn the basics of good advertising.

You will gain a better appreciation between the difference of Marketing and Advertising, learn how to get the most for the least investment and ensure that you do it all profitably.

Disc 5 in the Business Essentials Series
Maximising Your Conversion Rates

Get to know how your Sales Pipeline REALLY works and how to identify who your suspects really are, convert prospects into regular shoppers and understand how much more work you can do to maximise your sales experience.

Disc 6 in the Business Essentials Series
Meet and Exceed Your Clients Expectations

Now you have new customers, how do you make sure you KEEP them, how do you wanting to come back time and again while telling their friends? ...this is where you really make a difference.

Disc 7 in the Business Essentials Series
Systemising Your Business For Consistent Excellence

Do you recognise the importance of having systems in your business and how they can improve your profitability?

We show you how to systemise like a corporate while retaining the culture of a smaller business. Understanding how we systemise for routine and humanise for the exceptions will enable you to be the best in your field every time.

Disc 8 in the Business Essentials Series
Do You Have a Champion Team with a Champion Leader?
This is about having the right people on the bus. It starts with you however so you'll learn how to maximise your own skills and then you will attract and retain the right people.

When you understand how the TEAM is the most important part of your business and what needs to be done to achieve the very best from yourselves and others you are well on your way to becoming a better manager of this invaluable resource.

Disc 9 in the Business Essentials Series
The Essentials of Getting Your Time Back.
This is where you get to redefine your time management You will understand better how you can start working far more on the business than in the business than ever before.

You will also finally find out why others can seem to fit more into their day while having a great LIFE – WORK balance (notice the order!)..

Disc 10 in the Business Essentials Series
Simply Brilliant Customer Service.
It's so easy to give mediocre or good customer service but it's just as easy to give amazing service to your customers and delight them.

You will understand the simple easy steps that you must take to provide consistently brilliant service and how to get your team excited about doing it.

Disc 11 in the Business Essentials Series
Discovering DISC and EQ not just IQ.
We believe for things to change first you must change so here you will learn why you behave as you do and just as importantly understand why other people react and act the way they do.

You will also learn what DISC really is and what it isn't. You will learn how to apply these important principles in your recruitment and team management / development.

You will learn how to use these ideas in creating a more dynamic team and discover the what and why of emotional intelligence. You will also develop key strategies for using the knowledge here and the tools we have available on our website and why we place such a massive emphasis on DISC and other tools that support, train and develop your team.

You will also learn how to use these skills and observations at home and socially not just at the workplace.

Disc 12 in the Business Essentials Series
Quality Recruitment.
Recruitment of the right people for the right reasons in the right roles for your team is so incredibly important yet so often ignored or pushed to the rear.

You will learn who the right person is for your business and the role you want filled.
You will be able to identify the right people early in the process to save yourself and them the time and money wasted with antique recruitment methodologies that just don't work anymore.

How to get the best out of your recruitment activities so you can keep the assets you acquire for the long term and get the best return from your investment.

ABOUT THE AUTHOR

John Millar is the Managing Director, Senior Business Coach Trainer and Consultant with More Profit Less Time Pty Ltd and CEO-ONDEMAND. Along with his many other business interests, John is proud to have been an associate of the most successful coaching team in the world.

He is recognized as a global leader and has been benchmarked against over 1,300 colleagues in 31 countries. John has over 25 years of hands-on ownership, management, coaching, and entrepreneurial experience in a broad range of industry sectors, including retail, wholesale, import, export, IT, trades and trade services, automotive, primary production, food services, transport, manufacturing, mining, professional services, the fitness industry, and more.

He has extensive experience developing and providing training for small to medium-sized companies and a variety of publicly listed corporate companies. John is an accomplished and talented public and professional speaker. He has been a mentor working with sales/management activities for businesses with a turnover under $100,000 per annum, over $100 million turnover, and everything in between, with great success.

John currently works with business owners and their teams across Australia and has a "Whatever it takes" attitude that has enabled him to help his clients grow their business profits by up to 800%.

 If you are ready to be coached by one of the best in the business, register at:

www.ceo-ondemand.com.au

Make sure to visit www.moreprofitlesstime.com for the new online Management Development Program: The Business Essentials Series.

ACCLAIM FOR JOHN MILLAR'S
Business Coaching and Training in their own words…

"Without John Millar as my Business Coach I wouldn't have a business today."—Grant Jennings Managing Director, Jigsaw Projects

"Taking the decision to be coached and trained by John Millar was carefully considered after experiencing those who over promised and under delivered. I am pleased to say the content of his courses are the tools we all need to master as business owners. His delivery is engaging, thought provoking and empowering and after every session I came away re-energised. John always makes himself available for business building advice both via Skype and face to face beyond the scope of delivery. With his extensive personal experience in building small businesses, he knows and understands what it takes to establish and grow a business. I have no hesitation endorsing John Millar as an educator and business coach and the bonus is he is a very nice person."—Anne Lederman Managing Director FB Salons"

Johns training with my management team was excellent, it was very different from the business coaching and support I have had in the past. John was clear, thoughtful and he addressed the issues we needed to cover without us even knowing they were being addressed! His follow up has been fantastic and exactly what I needed. I would recommend John and his team to anyone looking at getting some business coaching and training done" —Wendy Crawford, Peopleworx

"In my dealings with John as our business coach, I have found him to be a motivated and insightful agent of positive change. He is able to burrow down to the root cause of issues and introduce effective forms of measurement. John then identifies and implements practical solutions and is there to provide the gentle persuasion required to ensure that results are achieved." —Mark Felton, Lindale Insurances

"You have coached and trained us so well throughout the year that we are now used to & find it easy to prepare a 90 day plan, then breaks it down to actionable bite size pieces. Planning in business & personal life certainly is important. It allows us to identify the important things & the bigger picture. Thank you for your support & guidance throughout the year. And not to mention your insight, external perspective to review & assist our business moving forward." —Linda Turner, Director Roy A McDonald Certified Practicing Accountants

"If you want to achieve sales results you never thought were possible and give yourself a competitive edge my strong suggestion is to engage John services and listen closely to what John has to say, during the time I was trained by John I was one of eight sales consultants in a national business for 10 out of the 13 months I lead the sales tally and in 1 quarter I generated three times the revenue of the national sales force combined. Johns training and experience was well worth the investment and paid big dividends. Thanks John." —Julian Fadini, Bellvue Capital

"John is a very enthusiastic trainer and business coach, he is very passionate about getting business owners and their team where they need to be. He goes the extra mile to keep ahead of the latest developments which he then uses to benefit his clients." —Darren Reddy CPA

"I have been to a few seminars and heard John speak numerous times about sales, marketing and business. He is a very knowledgeable and extremely enthusiastic business coach in all his interactions and I would recommend him to all business owners who need a sales and marketing boost!" —Andrew Heath, Managing Director, Fresh Living Group

"I worked with John Millar and found his business knowledge, passion and innovation to be inspiring. He has always been able to set (and achieve) strategic long and short-term goals both for himself and his clients without losing that personal connection he builds with everyone he meets. He has been and I believe will continue to be a strong mentor and trainer for anyone wanting to take that next step in their business." —Bree Webster, Online Marketing Guru

"Massive Action Day" – what an understatement, John Millars 4 hour frenzy challenged me to seriously review areas of my business I would not have gone to .... In this way, the process identified incongruence's in my mind, my business and my modus operandi. It's created a paradigm shift. Thanks John, the road map just got a whole lot clearer. Your friendship and insights since 2003 have been a gift to my business and I." —Andrew Reay, Counsellor, Hypnotherapist and Counsellor, Thinkshift Transformations

"John Millar is not your usual Business coach or trainer; he gets involved with you and your business and provides hands on help to make sure you follow through on his advice. He is highly motivated to help his clients and his personal guarantee certainly shows this. He has now transposed his thoughts, advice and love of good business onto a series of DVD's in his business venture – More Profit Less Time. This has excellent tips and advice for anyone either starting out or already in business. I highly recommend John to any business owner who wants to run a business and not a j.o.b.!" —Darren Cassidy, Managing Director HR2U

"I and many of my Business Partners and colleagues have worked with John since 2010 as our business oath, trainer and motivator and found him to be an extremely motivational person to assist us achieve our business goals. This company and its products allows for John's skill set to be accessed by a wider number of potential clients. His very professional DVD series is extremely good value for money and is easily accessible for all of us who are time poor. If you are looking to maximise your and your business's results and to start achieving your goals and dreams, contact John; you won't look back!!" —Mark Cleland, Mortgage Choice

"John develops real relationships with the people he comes into contact with. He is pasionate about what he does. His DVD and group training series, is full of good ideas and process to make your business better. Knowing what to do and actually doing it are two different things. John is excellent at helping you get things done." —Carey Rudd, Sales Director, Online Knowledge

"I have known John since 2004 and found him to be extremely knowledgably in both Sales and Business systems as a business coach without peer. John has provided me with business advice as well as personal coaching over the years, helping me with the running of my organisation. I'm impressed with John's DVD series where he has condensed a lot of the information in an easy to follow format that any business owner can use immediately. I wish he had released these DVDs earlier, as they are a goldmine of information, and practical how to that allow anyone to increase the profit in their business and get back valuable wasted time." —Steve Psaradellis, Managing Director, TEBA

"John's DVD and workbook delivery of his no-nonsense advice provides a low-cost option for those business owners looking to set and achieve goals that will increase profit. I found the conversational style of the DVD's easy to follow, whilst the requirement to pause the DVD and write down some action points ensured a level of commitment to the advice being provided." — Mark Felton, Lindale Insurances

"I only met John briefly at a BNI meeting and knew instantly i need to hire him for my business as my business coach. His attitude towards work and how to improve my cash line had an instant effect on before, even before I finally hired him on an official basis. I found myself thinking "what would John do" and this was only after just meeting him. I cannot see my business expend and give me "More Profit Less Time" without John's expert direction and training. If you want to succeed in business life, you need John Millar, without him you're just kidding yourself " —Leslie Cachia, Managing Director, Letac Drafting

"I can highly recommend John Millar to any business owner who wants to grow his business. When I hear very positive feedback from colleagues who are skeptics by nature about John's ability and skills, I know John will help all those he comes in contact with. John comes with a selfless nature and the willingness to work inside a client's business to make it succeed. Rare indeed!" —Darren Cassidy, Managing Director, HR2U"I first met John Millar in mid-2010 and have always found him to be of an honest and generous character that engenders an easy association with him. I love how easy he is to listen to and how passionate he is about his work and topics. John demonstrates a love for life and his work and I have no hesitation in recommending his services." —Kathie M Thomas, Managing Director, VA

"I have listened to John speak on a number of occasions and find him a very knowledgeable speaker with a passion for what he does. I have also interacted with a number of his clients and they all tell me that he helps them achieve results in their business. If you are looking for business help John is a person you can trust." —Carey Rudd, Sales Director, Online Knowledge

"John knows his stuff, he knows how the get results, John has so many great ideas in building a business and helping business owners work less and make more money. John has released a DVD set on doing just that. I have watched the 1st one and it was great, very informative and easy to understand, I happily recommend John to anyone in need of help and guidance" —Frank Eramo, Proprietor, Dynotune

"I have known John only for a short time, however the impact that he has had on me, not just my business has helped me to visualise opportunities that I began to doubt my ability to realise. He is encouraging and at the same time challenging so that he can/you can, begin to see how to maximise the business potential, John calls it being an unreasonable friend, I call it being a mate. If you have any questions about the direction of your business, if you want to seem your bottom line improve not just turnover but real profit, if you want a person who will work with you then I strongly recommend that you engage him at your earliest convenience. John is the best thing that has happened to my business. I could tell you about the way he is on track to make 1/2 a million for me on his contacts alone, but that actually sells him short, he has become like my partner in business, and cares about my success as if it was his own, we will flourish because I took the step to employ his training to help me grow. If you get a chance to get him training you, don't wait like I did, get in as quickly as possible, his time is your business and if like me your business is to make money, then every day you don't have him on retainer you lose money." —Russell Summers, Managing Director, The Give Life Centre

"It's usually easy to be mediocre in business but it's impossible when you have John Millar training you. He has been my right hand since 2003!" —David Manser, CFO, Hydrosteer

"I now have a commercial, profitable business and now it's my choice when I work IN my business and when I work ON it and have had john helping me in business since 1988. I can't imagine not having John as a part of our business." —David Wall, Director, D&K Transport

"The work John has done since 2008 coaching and training our marketing team, administration and finance teams, buyers, store managers and staff nationally have been fantastic." —Ross Sudano, Director, Anaconda Adventure Stores

"John is a creative, professional, practical and committed business coach and trainer. His approach since we first met him in 1994 to working with a client team through the application of useful tools, information and anecdotes along with his easy going & easy to understand delivery sets him apart from other business coaches that I have used in the past." —Anthony Beasley, Director, The Astra Group

"I have worked with John Millar for the since 2004 and I didn't think it was possible to achieve what we have achieved together. His business coaching, training and services just get better and better!" —Terrance Chong, Managing Director, Echo Graphics and Printing

"John's business coaching, training and support has transformed our business across Australia and New Zealand since 2008."—Rose Vis, Managing Director, VIP Australia

"We first met John in 2005, he is AMAZING at sales, marketing, operations, logistics, finance training and so much more. Since engaging John as our business coach our business has exploded, our team are happy, our clients are raving about us and my husband and I now take at least 12 weeks holidays a year, EVERY year." —Shirley Du, Director, Goldline Technology

"It's the no nonsense results driven business coaching and training focus John bought to the table that had such a massive effect on our business." —David Runkel, Director, Tracomp Fabrication and Steel

"We started working with John in early 2010, within 90 days of working with and being trained by John Millar we had the biggest and most profitable month in our 15 year history. That's impressive." —Hugh Gilchrist, Managing Director, Australian Moulding Company

"If you don't have John as your business trainer you aren't meeting your business potential." —Don Robertson, Director, Medallion Electrical Services

Thank You

www.ingramcontent.com/pod-product-compliance
Lightning Source LLC
Chambersburg PA
CBHW050402180526
45159CB00005B/2114